CORAL REEF FOOD CHAINS

by Rebecca Pettiford

pogo

Ideas for Parents and Teachers

Pogo Books let children practice reading informational text while introducing them to nonfiction features such as headings, labels, sidebars, maps, and diagrams, as well as a table of contents, glossary, and index.

Carefully leveled text with a strong photo match offers early fluent readers the support they need to succeed.

Before Reading

- "Walk" through the book and point out the various nonfiction features. Ask the student what purpose each feature serves.
- Look at the glossary together. Read and discuss the words.

Read the Book

- Have the child read the book independently.
- Invite him or her to list questions that arise from reading.

After Reading

- Discuss the child's questions. Talk about how he or she might find answers to those questions.
- Prompt the child to think more. Ask: What other coral reef animals and plants do you know about? What food chains do you think they are a part of?

Pogo Books are published by Jump!
5357 Penn Avenue South
Minneapolis, MN 55419
www.jumplibrary.com

Library of Congress Cataloging-in-Publication Data

Names: Pettiford, Rebecca, author.
Title: Coral reef food chains / by Rebecca Pettiford.
Description: Minneapolis, Minnesota : Jump!, Inc., [2016]
Series: Who eats what? | Audience: Ages: 7-10.
Includes index.
Identifiers: LCCN 2016028097 (print)
LCCN 2016045059 (ebook)
ISBN 9781620315736 (hardcover: alk. paper)
ISBN 9781620316122 (paperback)
ISBN 9781624965210 (ebook)
Subjects: LCSH: Coral reefs and islands—
Juvenile literature.
Classification: LCC GB461 .P47 2016 (print)
LCC GB461 (ebook) | DDC 578.77/89—dc23
LC record available at https://lccn.loc.gov/2016028097

Editor: Jenny Fretland VanVoorst
Book Designer: Michelle Sonnek
Photo Researcher: Michelle Sonnek

Photo Credits: All photos by Shutterstock except:
Alamy, 11, 14-15; Getty, 16-17, 20-21tm, 20-21bm;
iStock, 1, 19, 20-21t; SuperStock, 6-7, 20-21b;
Thinkstock, cover.

Printed in the United States of America at
Corporate Graphics in North Mankato, Minnesota.

TABLE OF CONTENTS

CHAPTER 1

··

RAIN FORESTS OF THE SEA

Coral reefs are one of the planet's most diverse and beautiful **biomes**. They are found in warm, shallow ocean waters.

Coral reefs make up less than 0.2 percent of the ocean floor. But nearly a third of the ocean's plants and animals live there. This is why they are called "rain forests of the sea."

coral polyp · · · · ▸

A coral reef begins with a single animal. A **coral polyp** sticks to a rock. It surrounds itself with a hard skeleton. Then it splits into many polyps. Each has its own skeleton.

A **colony** forms. Over time, the skeletons of the colonies grow together. They connect to form a reef.

It takes a long time for a reef to grow. It grows less than an inch (2.5 centimeters) a year.

WHERE ARE THEY?

Coral reefs are found along the coasts of East Africa, South India, Australia, Florida, Brazil, and the Caribbean.

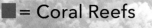
= Coral Reefs

CHAPTER 2

THE CORAL REEF FOOD CHAIN

All living things need energy.
Reef plants get it from the sun.
Animals on the reef eat plants
and other animals.

A **food chain** shows how energy moves from plants to animals. Each living link in the chain eats the one before it.

Plant plankton and sea grass are **producers**. They are the first link in the coral reef food chain. These plants use the sun's energy to make their own food.

Small fish and green sea turtles eat the plants. They are the next link in the chain. They are **consumers**.

DID YOU KNOW?

The Great Barrier Reef is in Australia. It is the largest reef in the world. You can see it from outer space!

parrotfish
(consumer)

sea grass
(producer)

octopus
(predator)

squid
(predator)

Large fish, octopuses,
and sharks eat consumers.
They are **predators**, the
next link in the chain.

Sharks are a top predator.
They eat smaller predators.

DID YOU KNOW?

A reef gives animals
cover. It helps them
hide from predators.

When an animal dies, **decomposers** such as **bacteria** break down its body. They change the dead matter into **nutrients**. The nutrients return to the sea floor.

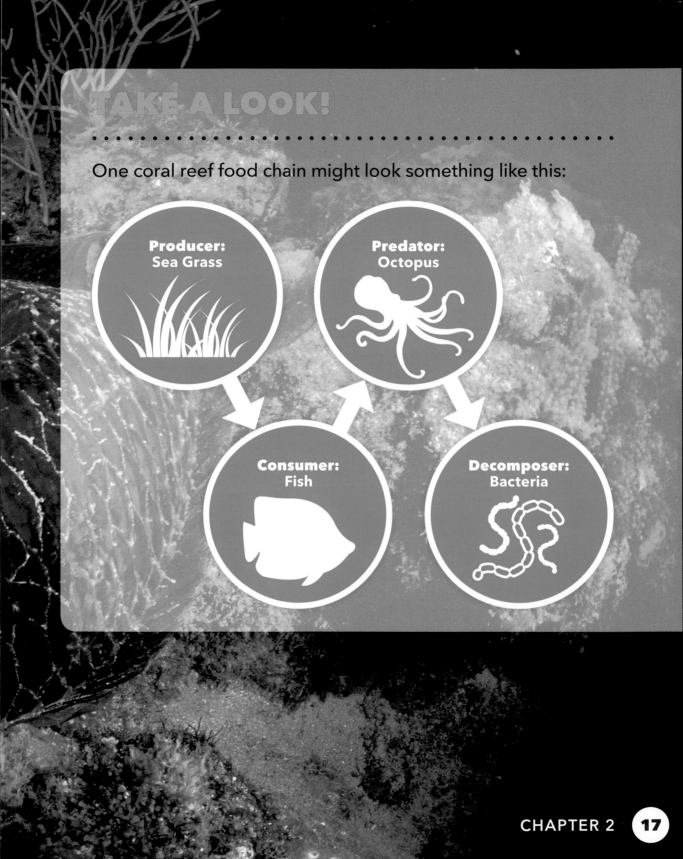

TAKE A LOOK!

One coral reef food chain might look something like this:

Producer:
Sea Grass

Predator:
Octopus

Consumer:
Fish

Decomposer:
Bacteria

CHAPTER 3

FOOD CHAIN CLOSE-UPS

Let's look at a simple food chain.
Sea grass grows on the reef.
A sea turtle eats the sea grass.

A shark eats the sea turtle. When the shark dies, bacteria break down its body.

Let's take a look at another food chain.

1) Plant plankton grows near the reef.

2) A sea sponge eats the plankton.

3) A fish eats the sponge.

4) An eel eats the fish.

In time, the eel dies. Bacteria break down its body. The food chain continues!

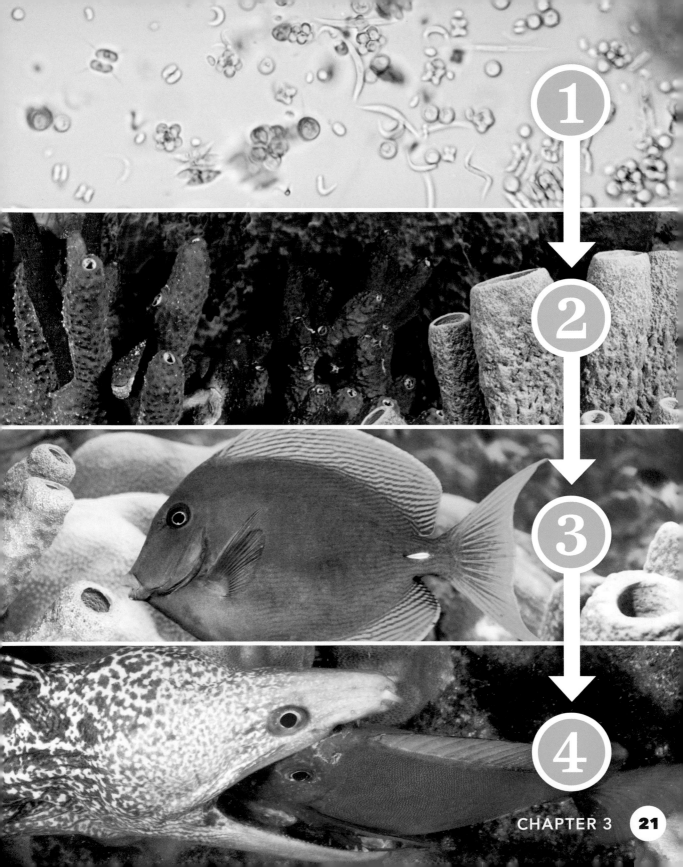

ACTIVITIES & TOOLS

YOU CAN HELP!

Coral reefs are in danger. Human activities such as pollution and overfishing are destroying them. You can help save coral reefs. Here are some ideas:

1. Save water. The less water you use, the less wastewater will pollute the oceans.

2. Walk, bike, or ride the bus. Burning fossil fuels like gasoline leads to ocean warming. This destroys the reefs.

3. Use organic fertilizer in your garden. Although you may live far from a coral reef, fertilizers can get into the water system. They pollute the ocean. This hurts reefs and the animals that live on them.

4. Do not litter. Do not leave fishing lines or nets in the water or on the beach. Litter harms the reef and ocean life.

5. Plant a tree. Trees help slow the warming of the land and oceans.

6. Do not touch the reef. Touching the coral animals will hurt them.

GLOSSARY

bacteria: Tiny life forms that break down dead animals.

biomes: Large areas on Earth defined by the weather, land, and type of plants and animals that live there.

colony: A group or community.

consumers: Animals that eat plants.

coral polyp: A tiny animal with a hard skeleton that forms coral reefs.

coral reefs: Ridges in the ocean that are formed by coral polyps.

decomposers: Life forms that break down dead matter.

food chain: An ordering of plants and animals in which each uses or eats the one before it for energy.

nutrients: Substances that are essential for living things to survive and grow.

plant plankton: Tiny ocean plants.

predators: Animals that hunt and eat other animals.

producers: Plants that make their own food from the sun.

INDEX

TO LEARN MORE

Learning more is as easy as 1, 2, 3.

1) **Go to www.factsurfer.com**

2) **Enter "coralreeffoodchains" into the search box.**

3) **Click the "Surf" button to see a list of websites.**

With factsurfer, finding more information is just a click away.